KNOCK,

NOCTURNAL

Who is There?

by Jeryl Christmas

This Book Belongs To

_____

KNOCK, NOCTURNAL
Who is there?

Fireflies

light the nighttime sky

competing with the moon.

A cricket

rubs its wings together

chirping his own tune.

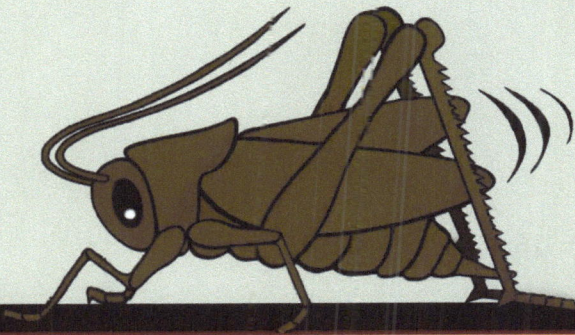

KNOCK, NOCTURNAL
Who is there?

A possum

knows a clever trick.

He likes to fake his death.

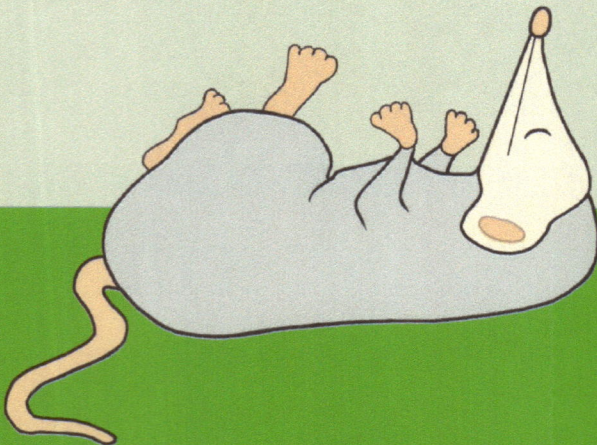

And if you

ever scare a **skunk**,

you better hold your breath!

KNOCK, NOCTURNAL
Who is there?

An **aye-aye**

has a finger that taps trees

to find his food.

A **hedgehog**

curls up in a ball

whenever he's pursued.

KNOCK, NOCTURNAL
Who is there?

Snails

retreat when faced with harm

and go inside their shells.

A **tarantula** spider

is a terror anywhere

it dwells.

KNOCK, NOCTURNAL
Who is there?

Great horned owls

float through the air

without a single sound.

A **badger**

spends his daylight hours

burrowed underground.

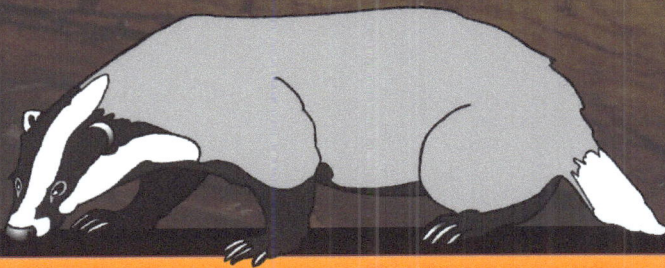

KNOCK, NOCTURNAL
Who is there?

Hyenas

"giggle" high-pitched sounds

that echo through the night.

Bats

use sound to navigate

when skies provide no light.

KNOCK, NOCTURNAL
Who is there?

Ocelots

don't chew a lot

but swallow their food whole.

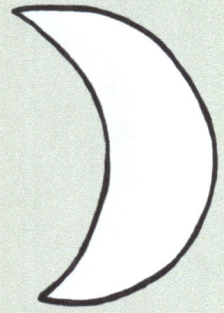

Coyotes'

cunning hunting skills

keep them in full control.

Rhino beetles

are quite large and hiss

when they're distressed.

A **drywood termite**

eats nonstop

and never takes a rest.

KNOCK, NOCTURNAL
Who is there?

A **beaver**

likes to gnaw on trees

and strip the branches bare.

The black fur on a

raccoon's face absorbs the

light and glare.

KNOCK, NOCTURNAL
Who is there?

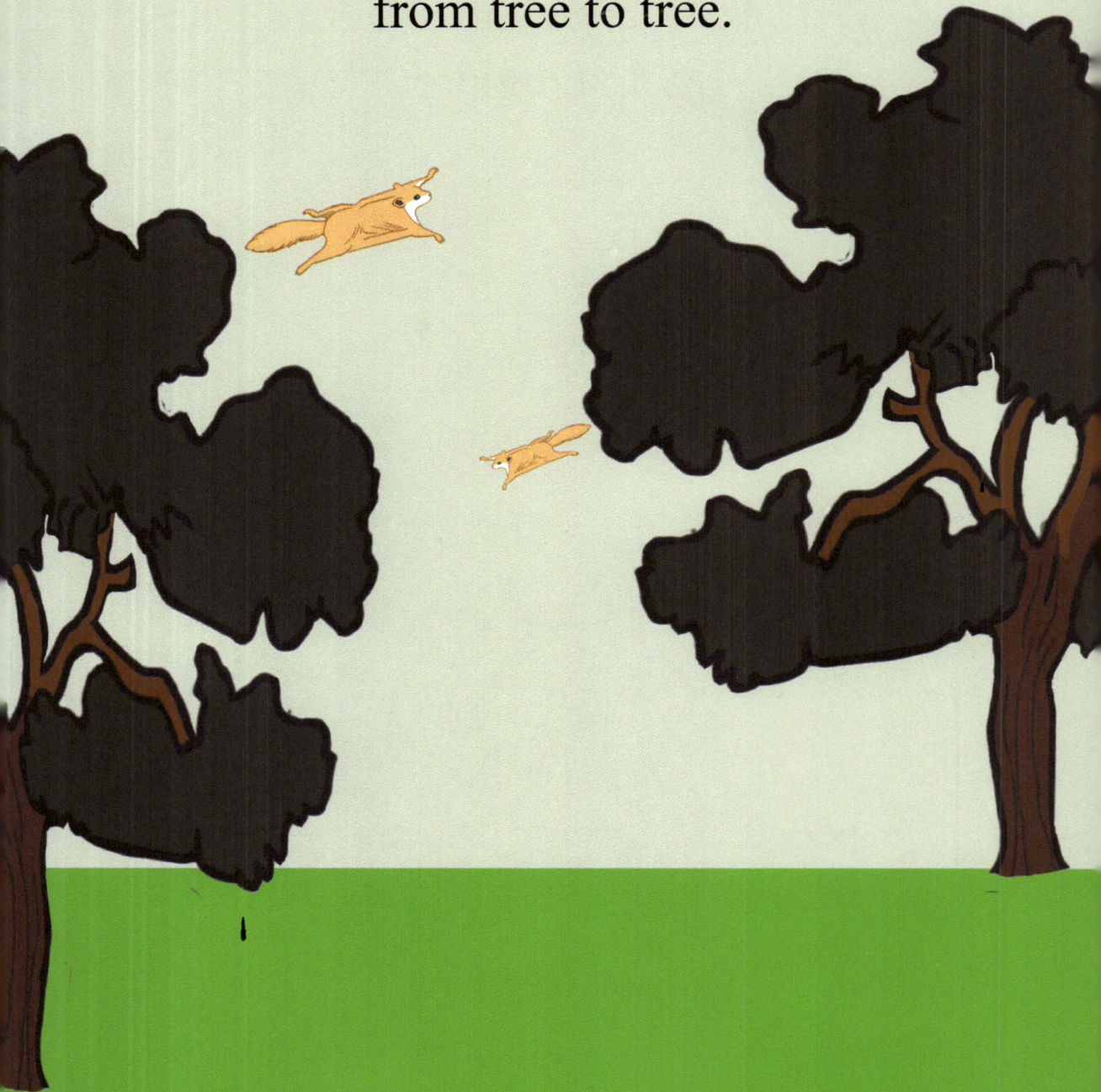

Flying squirrels,

like acrobats, can glide

from tree to tree.

A **red-eyed** tree frog

on a leaf is staring

right at me!

KNOCK, NOCTURNAL
Who is there?

Last, not least,

the **wildebeests,**

are suited **either** way.

They don't mind

spending time

out in the night **or** day.

THE END

KNOCK, KNOCK

Who's there?

Rita

Rita who?

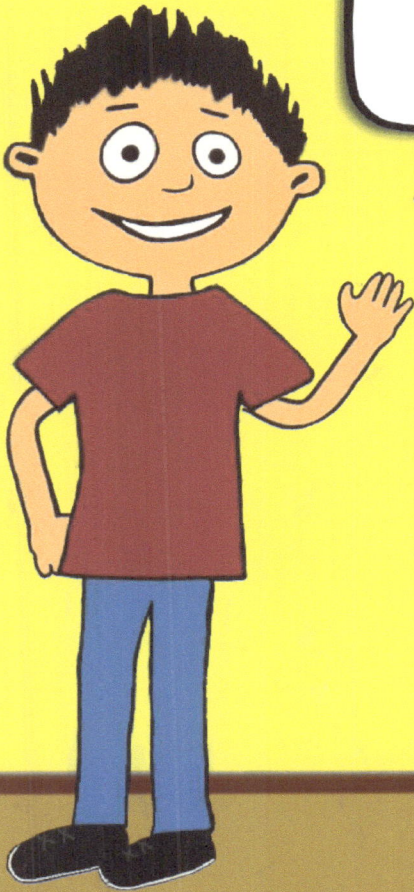

"**Rita**" book every day!

🐾 **Footnote:**
Nocturnal—active in nighttime
Diurnal—active in daytime

www.ingramcontent.com/pod-product-compliance
Lightning Source LLC
Chambersburg PA
CBHW060840270326
41933CB00002B/148